INSIGHTS OF A TRIAL ATTORNEY

A Practical Guide For Attorneys, Jurists, & People In Need Of Legal Representation

By **Martin V. Asatrian, Esq.**

Speakeasy Publishing
73-03 Bell Blvd, #10
Oakland Gardens, NY 11364
www.speakeasypublishinginc.com

Ordering Information:

Quantity sales. Special discounts are available on quantity purchases by corporations, associations, and others. For details, contact the publisher at the address above.

Orders by U.S. trade bookstores and wholesalers. Please contact Speakeasy Publishing: Tel: (888) 991-2766 or visit www.speakeasypublishinginc.com.

Printed in the United States of America

Published in 2021

ISBN: 978-1-954506-27-5

Foreword

I am writing this book to encourage others to do the same. I have always believed that philosophy and law have been interwoven. Here, there is a twist. The practice of law is in some ways a strange mix of psychiatry, philosophy, and sociology. Why this book is important is that it brings together a multitude of genres under the umbrella of the practice of law, in particular, the life and times of a trial lawyer. I hope some of you enjoy the book. It is not exactly a masterpiece but it is honest and comes from real life experiences. It may assist all professionals gain some insight in the absurdity of it all. Most importantly, I wrote this book for the underdogs in the world, and hopefully they can overcome obstacles and utilize some of my insights in checkmating even the most formidable adversaries. Fight to the death say, and the anthem here is always, a life on the bended knee is never a way to be free!

DEDICATION

This book is dedicated to the most important person in my life, my nine-year-old son, Benjamin Asatrian and Lisa Grazioso. There are however some honorable mentions, here we go; my father, Barkev, my mother, Arshaluis, my sister, Hasmik, my brother, Harout, sister in law, Diana Sarkisian, my brother in law, Movses Dovlatyan, and others. All members of my family, my nephew Anthony Asatrian, and all of my other nephews and nieces. I would do anything for my family, and even commit career suicide, the Asatrian blood runs deep in my veins, like my father, until they dip my casket I will never let anyone disrespect my family, cousins, aunts, uncles, you name it. I dare anyone to try it, you feel the wrath of ghosts of the Armenian Genocide and my struggles in the U.S.S.R., you can take my license, my money, but not my dignity, integrity, and especially honor. Death before dishonor! Bended knee is no way to be free! I also want to thank my friend Ernesto who showed kindness to strangers.

And others, I am almost fifty years old, and looking back in my life, I want to thank my childhood friends, my high school friends, college friends, and professors. Professional friends like Luigi Izzo, Eric Kahn, Frank Rodriguez, Andrew Moskovitz, Ken Javerbaum, Ben Morelli, Adam Deutsch, Connie Barrera, Lauren Kemp, Kristina Diaz Cooper, Jay Kanektar, Jeff Zajac, and others that have shown great support over the years. I do admire the kindness of Roman Abrahamovich, a great benefactor, and a crusader for antisemitism, and other selfless benefactors. I also want to thank all those I forgot to thank in this book, thank you to all.

DISCLAIMER

This publication is intended to be used for educational purposes only. No legal advice is being given, and no attorney-client relationship is intended to be created by reading this material. The author assumes no liability for any errors or omissions or for how this book or its contents are used or interpreted or for any consequences resulting directly or indirectly from the use of this book. For legal or any other advice, please consult an experienced attorney or the appropriate expert.

Asatrian Law Group, LLC
15 Warren Street
Hackensack, NJ 07601
(201) 663-3164
www.asatrianlaw.com

Table of Contents

I.	Foreword	3
II.	Dedication	4
III.	About The Author	8
1.	The Postmodern Critique	11
2.	The Deconstruction of Client and Attorney	17
3.	Synergy Between Client and Attorney	22
4.	The Limits of Representation	28
5.	Analyzing Adversaries, Understanding Judges	36
6.	Absurd Legal Outcomes	44
7.	Law And Philosophy	48
8.	Justice and Equality in the Courtroom	55
9.	Characteristics of a Quality Lawyer	63
10.	Conclusion	78
IV.	Acknowledgements	80

About The Author

My grandparents on my father's side came from a primarily Kurdish village called Kilice, which is in Turkey. My mom came from a village called Monash, which is also in Turkey. During the Armenian genocide in 1915, they essentially walked across the border to Aziz, a suburb of Aleppo, Syria (I guess you could call them a couple of the lucky ones), and settled in northern Syria. At the time, the Arabic and French leaders were told not to give Armenian refugees a hard time. Some refugees went to Syria, Jordan, Lebanon, and Egypt, while others eventually disbursed throughout Europe.

My grandfather's brother headed west in search of peace and tranquility, and ended up Brazil, where he became extremely successful making picture frames. My grandfather, on the other hand, encountered a lot of communist propaganda. "Why don't you join your Armenian brothers and sisters in the Armenian SSR?" he was asked. And that's what my parents decided to do; they went the communist route rather than the capitalist route, which was a big mistake. They settled near Yerevan, the capital of Armenia, which is where I was born.

When I was six years old, family in the United States invited us to stay with them. At that time, there was a treaty between Carter and Brezhnev, who was the premiere of the Soviet Union. We packed up and flew to Moscow, and then to Rome. In Rome, we were hosted by the Red Cross as refugees in the Soviet Union on their way to the United States. We were forced to stay in Italy to be "civilized" in a western European country before coming to the United States. The Red Cross put us up in a nice hotel (which I realize now was a refugee camp) and took very good care of us; for that, I will be eternally grateful to them.

I grew up in New Jersey, attended public high schools and grammar schools, and eventually went to university, which was an amazing experience. Prior to starting law school, I took a variety of courses at the University of Oxford and University of London, where I studied Shakespeare and philosophy. I eventually became an attorney, and have been practicing for 21 years now. I believe my unique background has shaped my work in many ways.

Why Write a (Third) Book?

The first two books I authored were autobiographical in nature, and explored what I've learned over the years about certain challenges that present to attorneys, and how to overcome them. This book is different in that it is more about a body of work, and about my observations as a professor of politics and law. It is intended for an audience of attorneys, jurists, and clients who might benefit from the strategies and insights of a trial and litigation attorney.

CHAPTER 1

THE POSTMODERN CRITIQUE

Postmodernity is not a flattering term; it's a term that refers to human beings as living in a virtual reality, where we are completely alienated from ourselves and others through the use of computers. In this state, the human being has been reduced to a robotic, automated entity that lives a superficial life and rapid existence. Immersed in a cycle of production and consumerism, the human being does not question the meaning of life or lack thereof; the human being exists merely to work (produce) during the day and consume during the night.

Postmodernity is a critique of that type of world…the type of world we are living in now.

The postmodern critique has its roots in the work of German philosophers like Friedrich Nietzsche and G.W.F. Hegel. Nietzsche marked the death of god, arguing that the state had replaced god and people worship the state. This was radicalized by the French Enlightenment thinkers and bankers of 1968 in Paris, where there were many riots and demonstrations.

One of the main tenets of this critique is that over time, words lose their meaning. Based on this sentiment, the postmodern radical thinkers went after the ancient Greek and Roman philosophers, arguing that since their works have been translated, it is impossible to understand their true meaning. On top of that, words take on different meanings over time.

While some people consider themselves to be an authority on Plato, Aristotle, and Socrates, supporters of the postmodern movement think that's completely ridiculous and absurd; how could one be an authority of something that happened 4,000 years ago, especially when there's no way to know what was lost in translation of the texts, and when much of the philosophy was oral? Critics of postmodernity were known to ruthlessly question all objective meaning, focusing strongly on logic and analytics.

To bring it back to law, there are certain principles that they espouse to which I can attest. One of these is a concept that the impartial individual does not exist; all interpretations of fact are subjective, and there is no such thing as an objective reality or universal truth.

In law, if someone believes that everything is subjective, then that means they believe that everyone brings to the table their own known and unknown biases, life histories, and dispositions towards individuals, whether with regard to race, ethnicity, gender, or orientation. To put it simply, everyone brings baggage to their interpretation of fact. For instance, a juror who has lobbies on known and unknown biases cannot possibly remain objective and make a complete, important decision on a murder case, for example.

The postmodern critique posits that a judge, lawyer, juror, or client cannot be completely detached, objective, and impartial. Rather, partial interpretations to a set of facts made by individuals determine the outcome of criminal, civil, and bench trials. The idea that impartiality does not exist can really shake the foundations of the legal system.

In New Jersey, there is an ongoing movement to train lawyers and judges to understand the sensitivity of their own biases and how they may impact their ability to handle a jury or bench trial. To be clear, this training is about raising awareness of personal biases and their impact on one's ability to make impartial, independent decisions in law; it is not about erasing one's personal life experiences.

The Acceptance of Biases in the Legal Realm

A lot of attorneys are aware that biases exist, and respond to the problem by saying something along the lines of, "That's just the way it is," knowing that they have no option but to work within the system. The issue is not just about the day-to-day practice of law where the presence and influence of biases may be overlooked, but about the ability to identify the problem. One cannot pretend that biases don't exist, whether it's in the context of a deposition, motion, or appeal; people have to recognize that dispositions toward life and certain classes of people exist, in large part because it can be very difficult for to people to understand worldviews that differ from their own.

Many people think that judges are impartial, and in fact, they are required by certain state laws to be impartial, and to disclose conflicts of interest so that there is no shattering of the public confidence of the impartiality of the jurist. For the most part, judges do their best to remain impartial and to weigh their personal biases. While it is impossible to be absolutely objective, judges aim to be as objective as possible. With an awareness of their biases, judges can make decisions that are fair, equitable, and in alignment with the law. In short, I have always had a positive experience with judges, and all lawyers should have profound respect for judges, and their commitment to justice, fairness, and equal distribution of justice. I have been fortunate to have encountered outstanding judges who are legal scholars and devoted to the truth, justice, and fairness.

Lawyers are advocates for their clients, and they are required to be diligent in their work product, which means doing the best they can for their clients within an ethical and moral framework. By virtue of the nature of their job, lawyers have to be partial in their zealous representation of a client. For that reason, they don't have to pretend to be impartial, and can bring to the table anything they want. This makes it easier for lawyers to deal with biases, whether they practice civil, criminal, or administrative law.

CHAPTER 2

THE DECONSTRUCTION OF CLIENT AND ATTORNEY

To Deconstruct a Client

To deconstruct a client is fancy way of explaining a process by which the attorney develops an understanding of their client. When meeting a client for the first time, an attorney needs to assess the client's facial expressions, mood, and agenda, as well as whether they will be an easy client to work with.

The attorney's goal is to ensure that a prospective client is hiring an attorney for the proper reasons, and that they have proper motives throughout the course of litigation. This is something that isn't always easy to do, because not many people will come right out and express their motives. A good lawyer will be able to assess the client's motivating factors and why they seek a favorable result in court.

The attorney should ask themselves, "Is this someone I could work with for the next two years?" If the answer is no, then the attorney will need to turn down that representation. An attorney needs to be extremely picky when it comes to deciding who they will and will not work for. The attorney should be able to effectively work with the client, no matter how trying and stressful litigation becomes.

No attorney wants to work with a client who only cares about the principle behind the case. If this is the case, the attorney should remind the client that it's not a moral court, but a legal court; it's not about moral principles, but outcomes. And outcomes aren't always fair, which is why there is an appellate division. An attorney should turn down a client who refuses to accept this truth, as those types of individuals are idealists, and no one—not even a perfect attorney—can satisfy the expectations of an idealist.

While an attorney is not a psychiatrist nor expected to act as one, they nonetheless have to deploy some psychological tools in order to make sure they are engaging with someone they want to work for, and that the client does not harbor ulterior motives, which could be damaging to the course of litigation.

For the most part, clients who seek the services of an attorney will be going through a very serious time in their life and are in need of something specific. They may be emotionally impaired, and not likely at their best. An attorney needs to understand and deconstruct this, as well as consider whether the facts of the case make sense and whether the case itself is winnable. That said, most clients are also cooperative and highly communicative. The attorney must speak the client's language and vice versa, especially in the post-COVID-19 age where communication is carried out primarily via text messaging and emails.

Law is not like buying milk from a grocery store; it is a time-consuming, cumbersome process that needs to be understood before it is undertaken. Through good communication, this can be conveyed to the client.

Another part of this process involves ensuring that the attorney takes a case for the right reasons. An attorney can always decline a case, but if they choose to accept a case, they need to identify the reasons behind that decision. Does the attorney believe in the client? Does the attorney believe that the case details fall within their area of expertise? Answering these types of questions is essential, as it is vitally important for an attorney to believe in the cases they take on. Deciding whether or not to take on a case is a pivotal decision that an attorney will have to make many times over during the course of their career.

To Deconstruct an Attorney

While the attorney deconstructs the client, the client also deconstructs the attorney.

Part of this deconstruction involves assessing superficial details, such as how the attorney and staff are dressed, how they greet the client at the door, and how extravagant or utilitarian the office space is. Why does the client want to retain one lawyer over another? Are they looking for an attorney who is a mechanic of the law, or an attorney who can get things done by being charismatic and charming? These are the types of questions that will need to be answered.

CHAPTER 3

SYNERGY BETWEEN CLIENT AND ATTORNEY

Synergy between client and attorney comes from a mutual understanding of the legal process, and acceptance of the fact that the case will be cumbersome, tedious, and procedurally-based. When an attorney and client are truly on the same page, great things can happen. There is a meeting of the minds between client and attorney, despite each having very different rights, roles, and responsibilities in the legal process. When this type of synergy has been established, representing a client can actually be a very fulfilling experience.

To be clear, there doesn't necessarily need to be a high level of synergy between client and attorney; it could be a low level of synergy based on a mutual understanding. Further, synergy is something that may develop or grow in intensity as the case progresses.

In essence, what is important is that the client and attorney see eye to eye on the more important issues, and that both view one another as a teammate. The lawyer is like the captain of the team—the one who makes decisions about procedural issues—while the client plays right alongside the lawyer and makes all of the other decisions. This brings to light the importance of making sure the client understands their role.

When a client and attorney work together in this way, they make a powerful team, accomplishing much more than either could on their own. This is especially true when considering the adversarial parties, who may not be operating as synergistically with one another. This is a problem that can be exploited through the strengthening of the relationship between client and attorney.

Synergy Doesn't Require Mutually-Appreciated Personalities

It's important to understand that the client doesn't need to like their lawyer from a personal perspective, and a lawyer shouldn't express any personal affirmation with the client unless it's just small talk. However, the client should respect their lawyer's work ethic and communication style, and feel confident that there are no divided loyalties. The client should also feel confident that the lawyer wants the best for them, and will make educated, professional recommendations.

Similarly, the lawyer doesn't have to like their client's personality; the lawyer's job is to be diligent in providing zealous representation and communicating with the client. While the lawyer doesn't have to like the client on a personal level, they should like and believe in the client's case.

Attorney-Client Trust

A lawyer should find their client to be believable, and trust that they are answering even very tough questions honestly. If a client is not completely truthful with their lawyer, it will complicate the case; in fact, lack of total honesty from the client is a good reason for the attorney to choose not to represent them.

If the lawyer feels that the client is not disclosing all necessary information, then they should have a discussion with the client about the importance of being transparent and providing all of the information they have. The client should understand how detrimental it can be for the attorney to be surprised by facts that come out during the case or during litigation, as opposed to beforehand. Failure to disclose all potentially relevant information can make matters highly complex, and even ruin a case.

From the lawyer's perspective, there is no such thing as an ideal situation, but it's definitely true that the lawyer would be better off representing a client who discloses everything from the start. In addition, the client should have realistic expectations and confidence in their lawyer's ability to handle the case. The client should have complete faith and trust in their lawyer, and if the trust is breached, the client should exit the attorney-client relationship.

Similarly, if the lawyer feels that their client is distrusting of them or lacks confidence in them, the lawyer should exit the attorney-client relationship, understanding that there may be nothing they can do to placate that client and ensure they are satisfied with the legal services rendered.

From my observations, trust tends to be an issue particularly with lawyers who work at large firms. Many people incorrectly assume that if a lawyer works at a big fancy law firm, they are trustworthy. In reality, the firm has nothing to do with it; trust is always about the individual lawyer.

Large firms often hire senior partners, but the clients never see them—they see a two-year associate instead, which is definitely not the same, especially when it comes to a case involving litigation. More and more, clients are realizing that just because a lawyer works at a large firm does not mean that they are of quality, nor that they hold a monopoly on the truth.

CHAPTER 4

THE LIMITS OF REPRESENTATION

To explain the limits of representation to a client, it's necessary to tell them in no uncertain terms that their case may be difficult. It will be difficult to try, and if it's an extremely difficult case, the likelihood of success is about fifty-fifty (although I would never put a solid number on it). The truth is that the facts of a case could go either way, and whenever there is a jury involved, it's always a roll of the dice. It will depend on the who the jurors are, and the county and venue where the case is being held.

The limits of representation must be made clear through the description of the scope of representation in the retainer agreement. This agreement should list the client's rights, the attorney's obligations, the rules of special conduct, and the framework for the representation. The client has to understand their responsibilities as a client, as well as the attorney's limitations.

The limits also have to do with the ethical framework within which one is dealing. The attorney cannot even come close to crossing an ethical line. In my experience, clients will respect an attorney who draws a clear line against any unethical acts. Of course, the attorney can keep secrets and confidences between themselves and the client, but they have to inform the client of what the professional rules of conduct allow.

The attorney should go above and beyond these rules in order to provide proper representation. In other words, the attorney can be extra diligent, competent, extremely sharp in their area of expertise, and zealous in their representation of a client.

Zealousness, which is a requirement of an attorney, goes back to the day of the zealous 4,000 years ago. Zealous is not necessarily a flattering term; it means to be fanatic. While an attorney has to be zealous, they cannot let their zealousness encroach on any ethical rules of conduct, and this is something the client should be made aware of. Zeal can be great, because it can mean having enthusiasm for and faith in a case. But zealousness has its limits, which are the rules of ethical conduct.

Part of keeping zealousness in check and practicing well within the rules of conduct is about remaining well-balanced; it means keeping zealousness in balance with the duties owed to the rules of professional conduct. Additionally, the attorney should cross-check themselves or counterbalance their enthusiasm for a case with practicality and rationality, which means limiting the client's expectations. It is an art that involves bringing both passion and logic to the table.

To be clear, I believe that as an attorney, it is important to embrace passion and emotion rather than fear it. This is something that has to do with the attorney's constitution, and in my case, it has to do with my love of the underdog in sports (a very American way of looking at things). I love the underdog, and feel compelled to advocate for them.

There is nothing more satisfying than being the David in David and Goliath. This is something that requires an enormous amount of skill, dedication, devotion, and personal time, but in the end, having passion for every single client and case is what tends to deliver good results. And at the end of a case, irrespective of the results, the attorney will know that they did everything they could for the client, which is a very rewarding feeling.

Managing Client Expectations

The attorney must consider whether their legal services are sufficient to satisfy the client's expectations. If the client's expectations are too high or too low, then the attorney may need to modulate those expectations, which is one of the most critical tasks an attorney must take on.

It's often the case that a client will have heard of an attorney's reputation as being "fearless," and will have high expectations as a result. However, the attorney has a duty to tell the client the reality and likely outcome of their case. The attorney must ensure that the client focuses not on the myths or rumors they've heard about the attorney, but on the facts of their case.

By delivering positive results early on in a case, a lawyer can actually become the victim of their own success. In other words, they can inadvertently inflate and elevate the client's expectations in various stages of litigation, turning a client who had very little faith into a client who has an enormous amount of faith.

Even if a lawyer has prevailed on a motion or certain discovery issues, it's important to refrain from doing a victory lap, because all litigation goes back and forth and has highs and lows. The highs provide a good opportunity for the lawyer to put the case in perspective and see the bigger picture, rather than focus in on small wins. A good lawyer will be keen to this and constantly modulate client expectations.

Working with the Unknowns

One of the most important things for the client to understand is that what might first be identified or perceived as a weakness in the case might actually turn out to be a strength, and vice versa. There will always be certain unknowns in a case, and the client must accept that. For instance, the client may be injured, but will not know the extent or value of their injuries until all of the treatment has been rendered and the outcome observed. The client has to be willing to show patience throughout their case, while many questions remain unanswered.

For an attorney, it's not easy to tell someone "I don't know," but it's vitally important to do so when indeed, the answer to a question is unknown. The point of civil discoveries, such as interrogatories, subpoenas, notices to produce documents, depositions, etc. is to gather more information, reevaluate the case, and hopefully answer the unknowns. Since facts and circumstances change, the initial evaluation of a case can change too.

The Elements Must Be There

When it comes to a personal injury case, at least three elements must be established: liability, causation, and damage.

Liability involves being able to show that one party was at fault for the damages. For example, in a rear-end collision case, can it be shown that the other party was at fault for the collision? Is there enough evidence to build a case against the defendant?

The next step is to show causation, meaning a causal connection between the collision and the damages. In other words, can it be shown that the rear-end collision was the proximate cause of the plaintiff's neck and back injuries?

Third, there must be actual damages in the case. No matter how strong liability or causation, a lack of damages for which to compensate the plaintiff can mean a very weak case that might not even be worth taking. The severity of the damages must also be considered. For example, has the plaintiff sustained permanent or long-term damage, or only minor injuries that will resolve within a few days or weeks? The greater the damages, the more valuable the case.

A personal injury client will almost always ask their attorney what their case is worth. Most good attorneys will not answer this question with a specific number early on, because it will depend on the treatment required and the outcome of that treatment. Without a determination of past, present, and future damages (e.g., the need for surgery and prescription medications in the future), there is no way to know the value of a case. This is something that must be made very clear to the client.

CHAPTER 5

ANALYZING ADVERSARIES, UNDERSTANDING JUDGES

In addition to watching the opponent as one would in a game of chess by analyzing and predicting their next moves, the attorney needs to pay attention to the adversary's personality before and during litigation. In general, there are three adversarial personality types that one can encounter in civil litigation.

The Arrogant Adversary

The arrogant adversary has an extremely high opinion of themselves; they will not only refer to but rely heavily on their prestige, such as the prestigious law school they attended or their prestigious family background. This type of person feels an enormous sense of self-worth and confidence, and will see themselves as someone who simply cannot lose.

A person who has this personality type is likely to encounter some major pitfalls, such as believing that they are much better than they really are, and therefore don't have to put in a lot of hard work. In addition, they might seriously underestimate their own adversaries.

The best way to deal with and ultimately prevail against this type of adversary is to remain focused on and diligent in completing the task at hand. Meanwhile, the arrogant adversary will be counting on their background to carry them to success, which isn't likely to happen, because every case requires a lot of hard work.

Attorneys who are up against an arrogant adversary should certainly avoid engaging in an ego yelling match or other behaviors which will only detract from the case at hand.

The Jekyll & Hyde Adversary

The Jekyll and Hyde personality type may be the most common, and is characterized by inconsistent behaviors. One day the attorney may be polite, cooperative, and easy to work with, and the next day they will be an absolute nightmare to work with. This is especially true if something in the case has not gone well for them.

This up-and-down personality pattern exists in a lot of lawyers and I've seen it many times throughout my career. It can be very difficult to deal with it, because there is no way of knowing whether it will be Jekyll or Hyde on any given day. The best way to deal with this personality type is to remain even-keeled, avoid getting pulled into the highs and lows, and remain focused on winning.

The even-keeled attorney can exploit the emotional instability of the Jekyll and Hyde adversary. They should be ready to see the adversary wearing one of many masks on any given day, or unmasked altogether.

The Renegade Adversary

The renegade adversary cares a lot about their clients and has complete faith in the legal system, but [1:00:44- 1:00:51 inaudible] violated their norms of justice. An attorney who has this personality type is unpredictable, which in law, can actually be a good thing because it keeps their opponents in the dark about their next moves.

It's essential to avoid getting caught up in the renegade adversary's unpredictability, or else risk losing control over the case at hand. The renegade adversary is difficult to deal with because not many things bother them; they're not reckless, but they are definitely fearless. They bring a lot to the table because they believe in and care more about their cases than most other attorneys. The renegade adversary is the most likely to be successful—not because they are geniuses, but because they believe in their cases and will work all hours of the night to prove them.

Judges—The 99 Percent

I work in multiple states throughout the country, which means I routinely deal with judges whom I know nothing about. In fairness to them, I always assume that they are balanced and completely competent in the law.

Over the course of my 20-year career, I would say that most—about 99 percent of—state, federal, and administrative judges are doing their best, are civil to the attorneys they deal with, and often have impressive wisdom and intelligence. These judges bring practicality to cases, resolving them in a manner that leaves both sides equally happy or equally unhappy, which is a sign of a good settlement.

Despite having seen it all, these judges bring fairness, equality, and equitable principles to the bench. I have an enormous amount of respect for these types of judges. In fact, a retired judge whom I once appeared before now works for my firm, and the hard work and fairness they bring to the table is invaluable.

Judges—The One Percent

Even the one percent of jurists deserve the benefit of the doubt. It's not easy being a judge—being in charge of ruling in favor of one party over another. No judge can get it right all of the time, which is why the appellate court exists. A judge is like a referee in a basketball game;

if they miss a foul or make a ruling based on an oversight, it can be appealed.

Judges have bad days too; they may be dealing with health problems, or may have just received news of a terminal illness. They may be cranky or distracted while on the bench, and having some sympathy for them with this perspective in mind can be helpful. It's important for attorneys to keep things in perspective and remain tolerant of certain behaviors.

That said, a judge has the power to sentence someone to decades in prison without parole. The decisions they make are incredibly impactful on individuals and communities. If a judge has explicitly engaged in inappropriate comments that violate the judicial code of conduct, or shown consistent behavior off the bench which indicates an enormous amount of partiality to one side (e.g., making rulings that are averse to one type of plaintiff 99 percent of the time), then the attorney will have some serious decisions to make.

Most attorneys will do nothing, while others will bring it to the attention of a presiding judge or make a grievance with the judicial apex committee in the given state. By doing something about it, the attorney is doing the right thing, and doesn't even necessarily have to conclude whether the judge engaged in judicial misconduct; they simply have to put it in the hands of the advisory committee.

Unless the potential misconduct is very blatant and affecting their clients' livelihoods, I believe attorneys should raise these sorts of issues sparingly. Some lawyers will choose to file a complaint against the judge, which could put a target on that lawyer's back and subject them to retaliation by other judges.

Alternatively, a lawyer will simply realize that they are in a negative situation, go to trial (and lose), and preserve all of the issues for appeal. If unsuccessful at appeal, the attorney can file a writ with the Supreme Court in the relevant state. There are certain judicial decisions that can be tolerated by the attorney and others that cannot; these are tough decisions that the attorney will have to make.

That said, attorneys should err on the side of not bringing a grievance unless it is very blatant, impactful, and violates the precepts of the law. Once a grievance has been filed, the attorney should not discuss it with anyone, but wait for the right people to make a decision, and hold onto faith in the system. I would say 99 per cent of the judges I have appeared before have been devoted to the law, are learned scholars, and their reputations are impeccable and honorable. And the remaining 1% may need sensitivity training, constructive criticism, and honor and respect that they deserve in the public interest.

CHAPTER 6

ABSURD LEGAL OUTCOMES

Even the most polished and seasoned attorneys get frustrated with the legal system. In today's climate of law, an attorney needs to assume that in every case, there could be a horrible outcome that defies the facts of the law. This is why attorneys should preserve every issue for appeal and make objections on record. In New Jersey, the attorney may need to utilize interlocutory appeals, which means taking the appeal before the case is over and asking for an emergency decision by the appellate court.

Even the venue can impact the outcome of a case, which seems absurd to a lot of people. Certain counties are much more favorable to defendants, while others are much more favorable to plaintiffs. This often leads to absurd outcomes that need to be addressed by judicial reform. If it's fair and just within one city's limits, it won't be fair and just in other city's limit, and this is something that needs to change.

When there's been an absurd or unreasonable outcome in a case, it's the attorney's job to sit down with their client and explain why the outcome was unfair and why there are grounds for an appeal. Under these circumstances, all the attorney can do for their client is file a motion to reconsider (which will be denied 99 percent of the time) and/or do the work to file an appeal. Fortunately, as long as the attorney assumed from the start that the case could result in an absurd outcome, then they will have already prepared the majority of the information necessary for an appeal.

Filing an appeal in response to an absurd outcome requires a lot of faith in the appellate courts. If the appeal fails, then the last option is to file a writ with the Supreme

Court in that state; the Supreme Court may or may not hear the case—they have no obligation to under the law.

Biases

If a case goes all the way to trial, there is the risk of a horribly negative outcome devoid of the facts and the law. In part, this is because the jury system is completely unpredictable.

For the most part, the jury system is a great system—probably the best system out there. However, it does have its flaws, weaknesses, and biases. Some jurists want to be on a case simply to rule against one party or the other, regardless of the facts of the case, which is a scary reality.

Jurists bring a lot of undisclosed biases to the table, and are liable to sway the opinion of an entire jury. It's critical to acknowledge that biases exist in order to work with them on a daily basis. One cannot raise the issue of bias haphazardly, but only when it poses a real and substantive problem.

Quite frankly, a lot of people could put their biases aside and do the best they can in ruling on a particular case. For example, if a municipal court judge lost a child to a drunk driver and was asked to rule on a drunk driving case, would it be reasonable to assume that they could put aside their biases and make a fair ruling on the case, or should the judge recuse themselves because of the personal issue they have? Not many people know about the personal lives of judges, nor should they, but something of this magnitude should be disclosed by the judge, because it could definitely impact their practical outlook on a defendant. Perhaps, a case of this sort should be handled via a bench trial or by a judge who has not suffered such personal trauma with the issue at hand.

Settlements

Part of the reason about 98 percent of cases settle is because both sides know that trial can result in imperfect and biased outcomes. To avoid this risk, many clients choose mediation or arbitration as a path to settlement, as this allows clients to weigh in on—to some degree—the outcome of the case.

CHAPTER 7

LAW AND PHILOSOPHY

Philosophy is a Greek word meaning 'love of wisdom,' and law is a subset of philosophy—a subset of the love of wisdom that involves manmade, black-and-white laws such as those in the U.S. Constitution, statutes, and regulations. The practitioner of law is tasked with understanding and applying these laws to any given case at hand.

From a philosophical standpoint, it's interesting to consider where law comes from. For thousands of years, people believed that the divine made the laws and passed on their powers to kings and queens, which then trickled down to the people. No one believes that anymore, and quite frankly, most don't even believe in or know how to feel about the founding fathers of the U.S. Constitution—the men who seemed to have two opposing sides to them, one of which owned slaves. Understandably, it can be difficult for people to reconcile these sides. Judgments regarding the founding fathers remains a big topic of discussion in universities across the country.

The philosophy of law poses questions about who makes the law and how they acquire the power to do so. To be extremely crude about it, the law has always been written by rich, wealthy people—the propertied and moneyed class. Most laws protect banks and corporations. They protect Walmart from shoplifters. Many laws are made by lawmakers who come from the elite class and whose only interest is to support the one percent of society. All laws are more or less rigged against the hardworking and the working poor.

With this in mind, it's important to bring some social justice elements into the practice of day-to-day law.

Certain philosophical assumptions have to be made, such as the idea that the law was made by people who protect the moneyed, connected, and elite class against the working poor.

Consider a large firm that's worth $20 billion. They have the most elite lawyers, and access to unlimited resources. Now consider that one of their lower-level employees has suffered gender discrimination and wants to file a lawsuit. Under these circumstances, how can the scales of justice be balanced?

It's going to be difficult—if not impossible—to find a lawyer who will go up against a huge firm or corporation, and as a result, corporations tend to get away with murder, and get away with treating their employees however they want; they know that they could crush any employee who creates a problem for them, and oftentimes they do. On the other side of that coin, most employees know this and have a fear of it, so they choose not to go after their employers at all.

This may be a jaded perception, but I believe it's a realistic one. Since the Industrial Revolution, lawmakers have been making laws that go against workers and unions. There has been some progress that's benefited the working class, such as workers' compensation and disability insurance, but the majority of laws have always been pro-bank, pro-corporation, and pro-state.

Existentialism

Existentialist ideas go against those of the Ancient Greeks, like Plato. Plato believed that life is all about the essence of life. But Jean-Paul Sartre and other philosophers argued that existence precedes essence, meaning that a person must exist first in order to have an essence in their life.

Existentialism suggests that one can tailor their life any way they want; there is no pre-determination, and no essence without existence. There are two ways of looking at the world: the first is to see life as full of meaning, and the second is to see life as completely absurd, meaningless, chaotic, and random.

Existentialists are interesting because they ask a lot of questions which they can't answer themselves, such as, "What does it mean to be a human that can choose from a multitude of options and sculpt themselves however they choose?" This question is at the crux of existentialism.

Many people don't subscribe to existentialism because they don't want that type of responsibility over their life. Believing that one is completely free to do whatever they want with their life leads to the question, "What am I going to do?" and most people can't answer that question—including existentialists.

In Albert Camus's 1942 essay, The Myth of Sisyphus, Sisyphus must constantly roll a rock up a mountain, only for it to roll back down again. This is an analogy for life, and Camus writes that the goal is not to worry about getting the rock to the top of the mountain, but about enjoying the process itself. This is an existential value that I respect and love: enjoy the day-to-day process, regardless of the outcome. The outcome will come, and even if it doesn't, it was only ever about the journey, not the end game. So many people have reached enormous heights, all along longing for the outcome rather than enjoyment of the process.

This ties in to the topic of the previous chapter, namely absurd legal outcomes. These outcomes happen when the law counters all of the facts and reason of a situation, puts innocent people in jail, and leaves significantly damaged people without any compensation or sense of justice.

Unfortunately, injustices happen every single day. Often, they take the form of an innocent defendant who cannot afford proper legal representation pleading guilty in order to avoid the consequences of a full-blown trial within a system they don't trust. The sad result is that many innocent people end up being sentenced to years or decades in prison.

Existentialism asks fundamental questions, even if they cannot be answered. Is life meaningful? How can one make their life meaningful? Have I made the right decisions in life, and can I change? Existentialism is also very practical, because it applies to everyone. It applies to the person in a cubicle at Morgan Stanley wondering why they chose to work in finance, whether it was the right decision, and what they can do about it.

Humans endure existentialist questions all the time. Ultimately, people can't just have a willful blindness to these questions, but should try to answer them no matter how difficult that may be.

CHAPTER 8

JUSTICE AND EQUALITY IN THE COURTROOM

Justice is an elusive word that means a lot to a lot of people. Justice always requires a degree of fairness and equity, which involves having sympathy and empathy for others, and promoting fundamentally fair outcomes (not absurd ones). To distribute justice, one must be blind—seeing all people as equal and treating them as such. Equal treatment under the law is a nice expression, but practically speaking, it's a bit too idealistic.

A billionaire could literally buy a law firm, put 100 attorneys on a case, and paper the other side to death by dropping 8,000 documents on them. This is something that the law does not address; the law does not say that the parties to a lawsuit must have equally competent legal representation. If one side has 20 attorneys working on a case day and night, then they are going to win, regardless of anything else. This is where justice gets pushed aside and the doors of the courtroom do not open equally to all defendants and plaintiffs.

The status of an individual may truncate the concept of equality in the courtroom. Imagine if a poor employee at Apple tried to take on Steve Jobs in the height of his wealth and power; there is no way Steve Jobs would have lost, because he was highly competitive and bright, and had an enormous amount of resources. One side will always have the upper hand.

There is no equal treatment under the law when billionaires are treated preferentially to the working class plumber. Judges know who the billionaires are, how much political weight they carry, and how many people are in their 'network.' In fact, a judge may even have to interact with the people in a billionaire plaintiff's network, which is problematic in that it impedes true equality under the law.

How can an individual who has no money defend themselves against a truck that's coming at them at 100 miles per hour with 7,000 pounds of force? They can't. And unfortunately, this is a good analogy for a situation wherein an individual goes up against a giant corporation, or even when a low-net-worth individual goes up against a high-net-worth individual.

Since the person with the most resources will almost always win, there is no such thing as equal treatment under the law. Simply put, this is because the person with more resources will be able to hire better attorneys, investigators, experts, engineers, and anyone or anything else necessary. That's how cases are won; money drives success in a legal case.

Justice in the courtroom does not take into consideration people's resources, wealth, and political connections, which are very important. The role of the court—whether state or federal—is to impose as much fairness and equality into a case as possible. When the court overlooks—either intentionally or unintentionally—the factors creating an unfair playing field, inequalities result. Judges play the role of a referee, but they also have an implicit power of equity, which means that they can bring in other factors like fairness, equality, justice, and manifest injustice into the equation. If these powers were to be employed, it would balance some of the inequities between a very wealthy plaintiff and a very poor defendant.

Addressing Inequality

To address inequality in the courtroom, my first suggestion would be to create a commission that studies the following:

(1) Whether or not biases play a role in the courtroom;

(2) what kind of negative impact they play;

(3) how to make judges more accountable for their decisions; and

(4) how to expand the equitable powers of judges (i.e., allow them to invoke fairness with the law to bring

more equality to the courtroom via affirmative acts rather than reliance on the black letter laws).

I would contact the legislative branch for judicial reform and the advisory committee in the Supreme Court to discuss ways to enact measures to restore equality in the courtroom. Injustice is inherited, and while some efforts are being made to address them, I believe greater efforts could be made. Compared to judges who have been in the field for over 25 years, younger judges are bringing a different worldview and deeper understanding of diversity to the table, which has been powerful.

In New Jersey, judges are appointed by state centers, which I belief is acceptable and even superior to the election of judges. That said, I believe more input is needed from laypeople in the community as to who will or will not be nominated for a judgeship.

I believe it is up to the judiciary committee to ask judges the very tough questions about the cases they have handled and how they have handled them, rather than simply rubber-stamp judges. Judges should be questioned as to how they are going to enhance justice in the courtroom.

When Money Talks in the Courtroom

Judges may not literally be "paid off" by one party or the other in exchange for a particular ruling, but that doesn't mean that more sophisticated influences don't exist.

Judges associate with other judges, and are not encouraged to associate with lawyers who will bring cases before them. Most judges come from the working class, although some come from an elite class and have elite circles.

Regardless, every judge can carve out their own world and bring certain unfair dispositions to the table. But regardless of whether a judge comes from a working, upper-middle, or elite class, they need to receive better training in sensitivity towards diverse populations (i.e., people of a certain gender, sexual orientation, etc.).

Public Confidence in the Judicial System

Judges need to understand that a litigant has nowhere to turn aside from the courthouse, and if a litigant is unfamiliar with the process and system, then they will naturally expect complete fairness from a jurist. Unfortunately, they will almost always be in for a serious shock when they realize that jurists are explicitly and implicitly unfair.

People talk about democracy and freedom, which in time, most people will come to realize are empty words. To discover this during a first-time encounter with the legal process can be devastating, especially when someone's livelihood is on the line.

This type of experience can shake a person's worldview, which is why it is important not to completely shatter public confidence in the judiciary. Part of this means not putting judges in a negative light when they are simply trying to do their best to deliver impartial rulings and justice.

That said, there also needs to be a certain level of accountability, because if a judge becomes too extreme and begins ruling against certain parties on a consistent basis, this could create enormous amounts of dissatisfaction and loss of confidence in the judicial system, which is the fabric of our country.

If people feel like they can't get a fair day in court, that's going to lead to what many call "anti-justice." It is extremely important to have a courtroom with a judge who is trying their best to be impartial and fair to both sides through an employment of their powers of equity.

CHAPTER 9

CHARACTERISTICS OF A QUALITY LAWYER

Not (Only) Focusing on the Benjamins

Just because a lawyer is motivated by money doesn't mean they are an unethical or incompetent lawyer. A highly diligent, confident, and ethical lawyer can look at a client and see a dollar sign on their forehead, and as long as they are getting good results for that client, the client isn't really going to care.

The problem with making it all about the money is that it does take away from the lawyer's motivation to become the best lawyer they can be, to engage in continuing legal education, and to never stop conducting their own research, because the law is constantly changing.

If a lawyer is constantly making efforts to build their knowledge base and sharpen their writing and negotiation skills, then the community will recognize them as someone who seeks excellence in the law. This will attract quality clients, which will result in higher legal fees and more billable hours (i.e., more Benjamins!).

While it is absolutely fine for a lawyer to be motivated by money, that cannot be their sole motivation. Chasing after money as the only goal is a trap for many lawyers, and an unsatisfying one at that. If a lawyer remains focused on being the best they can be, the money will follow.

Taking Chances, Living Dangerously

When going up against some of the most serious courts and heavy-hitters in the country, I would encourage most attorneys to be bold, and to take chances. Not only is this fun, but it will bring an enormous amount of enthusiasm and passion to the case, no matter the adversary.

All attorneys have gone to law school and been licensed equally to practice law. Attorneys shouldn't let big names and firms intimidate them; instead, they should feel encouraged to work harder to provide their clients with the best representation possible.

Friedrich Nietzsche, one of my favorite philosophers, said in his dying days that, "It's important to live dangerously as opposed to living safely." What he meant by that was not to cross the street without looking both ways, but to take chances in one's life and profession, and to innovate. Nietzsche—who became famous only after his death—loved the idea that an average person could develop superhuman skills in the form of an iron will and a fierce intention to carve out one's own life. This sentiment is why existentialists like Nietzsche; he supported the idea that a person can craft their own life and do what they want with it.

Nietzsche also talked a lot about passion versus logic, and how people need to bring both into their life.

Living dangerously could simply mean not taking the safe way, because oftentimes what appears to be safe isn't actually safe. If someone is constantly pushing the envelope within the limits of their own profession, then they are living dangerously in the sense that are going to be bringing a lot of negativity towards themselves. Living dangerously, in the sense that Nietzsche meant it, can revolutionize the practice of law, because it means thinking outside of the box, creating new ways to move into other areas of the law, and taking into account the philosophical background of law.

Never Quitting, Never Hesitating

What I learned from my days of playing sports is that I had to play until the very last second, and sometimes even had to go into overtime. As an attorney, I see this as a metaphor for never quitting on a case or client. The client will be watching every move their attorney makes, and if that attorney puts in 100 percent effort and never quits, the client is going to see that, and they will know that there are certain outcomes that simply can't be controlled. There is only so much an attorney can do.

An attorney's adversaries should see that they are not a quitter, and are going to constantly fight—not for the sake of fighting itself, but for the sake of equality and justice. This means taking an issue to the highest levels of every court, including the appellate division, state supreme court, and U.S. Supreme Court. This doesn't make the attorney a sore loser, it simply demonstrates the attorney's willingness to work with what the law permits, which is to appeal cases to the highest courts. In fact, some of the greatest cases have been decided by the highest courts, and by virtue of attorneys who never quit and never hesitate.

To "never hesitate" is instinctual and attorneys have to be careful with this, but sometimes it's necessary to follow instinct and to follow the basic essence of one's self. If an attorney feels that something just isn't right about a case, then they're probably right and should follow their instincts, and do what they need to do without hesitation.

Hesitation and uncertainty are philosophical norms that I don't subscribe to. I believe that hesitating is a problem from a life standpoint. Seizing opportunities involves not waiting too long and not overthinking, and this is where the concept of never hesitating comes from.

Learning from Loss

I have never met a seasoned, well-respected lawyer who hasn't seen defeat; no attorney will win every single case, but they also won't lose every case. When a lawyer loses a case, it doesn't necessarily mean they did a poor job handling it; in fact, it may be quite the opposite. An attorney cannot create or change the facts of a case, or create a jury pool that will decide in their favor.

Often, the reasons for losing a case are circumstantial. For instance, the lawyer's client could provide horrible testimony and lose their case by not following proper preparations prior to their testimony. Alternatively, the other side could just have a lot of facts in their favor during the late stages of litigation. There is always going to be some degree of randomness present. That said, a lawyer who loses a case should examine whether they did make a mistake or could have improved their representation in some way. Learning from losses will increase the chances of winning future cases.

Accepting that the Easy Way Doesn't Go Far

I fully believe that when a lawyer takes the easy way, they won't get far. The best trial lawyers tend to engage in a lot of solitude, self-improvement, and self-entertainment. This differs from the concept of trial lawyers associations, which is that trial lawyers should get together to share their crafts, stories, and lessons for becoming better at what they do. However, upon further examination, a trial lawyers association is really just a pool of politics; secondary to this is the actual exchange of ideas and opportunity for professional growth.

Just like any college club or debate team, things become political in trial lawyers associations. Members seek power and status rather than an enhancement of their skills and knowledge. Being president of a trial lawyers association can be lucrative for an attorney and their firm because it is a great designation to have. However, being president of this type of association also requires doing something for other trial lawyers, like protecting the attorney-client privilege and truly representing other trial lawyers rather than one's own personal desire to attract money, power, and status.

Unfortunately, many people in federal and state bars are only after power and status, and don't have a true intention to improve the profession and help other lawyers. In general, I believe that county bar associations and state trial lawyers associations fail in their purpose and stated goals. This is disappointing, but it's life.

Very good trial lawyers do extra reading and writing, and spend a lot of time alone. Of course, they also converse with fellow colleagues, but for the most part they focus on deepening their understanding of human psychology, sociology, and public perception.

Being Authentic

An attorney has to be true to themselves, know their values, and identify what they're willing to fight for until the very end; this is what it means to be authentic. Far too many attorneys make the mistake of pretending to be someone or something they are not.

The authentic person cannot be unmasked, because they've already unmasked themselves by being authentic. Authenticity doesn't mean simplicity; it means finding one's own voice and not relying on a false representation.

People who project their true selves into their work tend to be better at what they do, because they are embracing their values and strengthening their integrity.

When someone loses their integrity, they become compromised, which is when other people can more easily impact their thoughts and behaviors. These people are likely to conform to what others are doing, assuming it won't hurt their career. In reality, it will hurt their career because it will prevent them from changing or revolutionizing anything. These individuals become one with the herd—a mediocre person rather than an exceptional "superhuman," to refer back to Nietzsche.

Without being authentic, a person cannot build the bridge between mediocrity and greatness. When a person is completely authentic, they will have access to their inner genius, which is a Nietzschean concept that involves a chaotic and creative dimension. I believe everyone has an inner genius, but many people will never find it unless they allow themselves to be authentic. Some people go their whole lives never being authentic, but merely being what others want them to be. They might realize this only on their death bed, when it's too late.

Meditating, Exercising, and Living Within One's Means

At my office, we turn off the lights and meditate every single day, even if it is only for five minutes. This practice has a way of energizing the whole day, and it's amazing. Shutting down the brain via meditation gives the mind the ability to be creative like a god, and I think this is something everyone should do.

It's also important to be physically fit, as a healthy body makes for a sharp mind in the courtroom. I would seriously encourage weightlifting, boxing, and self-defense.

I would also strongly encourage people not to live above their means by trying to translate their success as a lawyer into material items, like an extremely expensive car, house, or vacation. I call this the "Facebook problem," because it's about people wanting to show off how great their lives are, and not admitting to any negativity or hardship. This is a myth.

Lawyers who gain some financial success and go that route will find out that law is really not a very lucrative practice; lawyers aren't tech giants making millions every day, they are middle-class people making decent hourly wages. It's important to keep this in mind and not rely on material possessions to reflect on a level of success.

Too many lawyers live a consumerist lifestyle and show off their expensive possessions as a way of projecting their worth. But in reality, lawyers don't make enough money to support the lifestyles they often boast. Further, doing this can subject the lawyer to becoming compromised and a slave to their practice. Lawyers should live a minimalist lifestyle but be awesome in what they do and constantly improve their skillset as an attorney. To live within one's means it just one way of being authentic.

Working Toward Personal Goals

Living a happy life with family and loved ones is a goal in and of itself. The life purpose of a lawyer could be different than the aims of a particular client's purpose. In every case, an attorney should do everything they can within the limits of their power to achieve the best results for their clients. However, an attorney may have a loose concept of their goals and purpose, and that won't necessarily affect their ability to practice law. In fact, not having rigid goals may actually make an attorney a better advocate, because personal goals and purposes could, in some cases, outweigh the interests of the client and swell into the attorney's law practice.

Unfortunately, the law is a rigorous practice and attorneys have to devote so much of themselves to their clients. So, when an attorney does have personal free time, what they choose to do with it is not necessarily going to impact their ability to do a good job for their clients.

Predicting Future Trends

My diverse background has benefited me. Having been born in a country that no longer exists (i.e., USSR) is a good thing. In one sense, I'm a US citizen, but I come from a global citizen standpoint since my family moved country-to-country and continent-to-continent in one lifetime, which not many people do. These experiences have allowed me to anticipate what's around the corner, whether it's good or bad.

By virtue of living such a full life, I am also better able to spot emerging trends in the legal field. I would say that on a day-to-day basis, the courtroom is becoming less available to the common working man, who is not going to have the same rights and legal costs as the extremely elite person.

I believe that a lower-level court for the average common person to express their grievances will be created. Quite frankly, some judges are intrigued by corporate battles [2:15:25-2:15:29 inaudible], and they're tired of the landscaper suing the owner who doesn't pay them—they're bored of these cases because they happen over and over again. I think a court will be created that's just for the average person, and they're not going to be allowed into the county courts or federal courts. I think that's an injustice because that's really going to change the way people do things. I think arbitration and mediation are good trends and I think that's going to happen more often, and I think there's going to be a cap as to how much money the average person can obtain in a courtroom, while there will be no cap for the corporations because they will be doing billion-dollar transactions.

In the future, I see less and less access to the courthouse by the average working person, as well as corporations using the courts and litigation as leverage for mergers, acquisitions, or other business motives. The corporate world is already dominating the insurance companies, and before long, it is going to dominate the courts and put individuals into small mediations and arbitrations with a cap.

As far as clients and their grievances are concerned, I think that they're going to have a gross mistrust and gross lack of confidence in the court system, because they're not going to have a stake in it. Unfortunately, people are going to realize that the courtroom will not get them justice, which is scary.

Many philosophers and legal scholars have said, "If you can't get justice in the courtroom, where do you go to get justice?" This is how organized crime and vigilante justice came about, where people take matters into their own hands and create their own justice. That is a horrible end game that people won't actually appreciate. No one wants to fight someone over a car accident at the point of the accident—that's ridiculous. But when money doesn't matter, whoever has physical strength at the car accident scene will win. It seems absurd, but I see it all the time.

Many people don't believe that they can get justice in the courtroom, so they take justice into their own hands. Even though this is the worst possible situation, I believe it is going to happen more and more. There will also be more organized or disorganized protests. The greatest threat to democracy occurs when people don't have access to the courts. I believe that our democratic ideals and ethics are going to go out the window in the next 20 years.

CONCLUSION

The true heart of this book is about merging my philosophical background and love for German and French philosophies with the practice of law. In trying to become the best advocate I can be, I have connected many philosophical precepts with my knowledge of the law. Some people choose to connect their faith with their practice of law, but I chose philosophy. I am always reading books on philosophy—whether it's Hegel, Nietzsche, Marx, or French philosophers like Derrida and Foucault—and always drawing from their wisdom.

Much of it is impractical, but some of it is practical and can be implemented in daily life, such as the idea that we can sculpt our own lives, as well as create justice for clients when the social norms won't provide it. Concepts of subjectivity and inclusive and exclusive biases also come into play during cross-examinations, because remaining constantly aware of what shapes people's testimonies can make for an effective attorney advocate.

Lastly, I would like to strongly suggest that lawyers bring something to the table other than the practice of law. For instance, a poet should bring some poetry into their practice of law; an artist should bring some artistic creativity into their practice of law; and a computer or electrical engineer should bring some structural knowledge into their practice of law. Bringing in elements that aren't strictly related to the practice of law makes for a better, more well-rounded lawyer, and also lends itself to a greater perspective that many lawyers just don't have.

ACKNOWLEDGEMENTS

What is a blueprint? It is a piece of paper with plans to make something on paper into something great. I feel that is what this book brings to light. My insights as a trial attorney come from my life on the playground, on the soccer field, classrooms, night clubs, and a cumulation of my life. I know as an attorney I give it my all like athletics, I fight hard, hustle, scrap, use skills, mind games, whatever it takes to win, but always play within the rules. But when I leave the courtroom, I do not hold any grudges against lawyers, judges, juries, and clients. But to crack the code as it were, you must have the confidence to look at your opponent, a lawyer, a judge, anyone, and say I will get the best of you, I will work harder, smarter, and will never quit. While you are playing golf, I am sharpening my craft, while you are tasting wine, I am taking your clients, while you are on vacation, I am always networking. You cannot beat a guy like me, tough, smart, persistent, and dare I say fearless. My goal is a simple one, never rest until you have achieved the highest honor which is being a billionaire. Why not? I met a few, not impressed, but they have something most do not, an engine, a drive, a thirst, to have it all. That I love in them. It is humane, all too humane, that is why I sleep three to four hours a day. I despise myself for not being more driven, more aggressive, more hungrier, and taking full of risks. But, I am getting close. If you shoot high and fail, it is ok. You tried your best, or did you? Look in the mirror and be honest for once in your life. You are not good, not as good as you think you are, to be elite. You must first think you are elite, a god, then you need a blueprint, and then you need to execute. Nietsche got it right, but never saw a single book sold. He knew we are all superhuman but we are afraid to be authentic, we are sheep and love our mediocrity. Wait for Blueprint IV. By then, I will be closer to hitting a Billion. Get rich or die trying!

NOTES

Look I cracked the code already. What are the odds of a refugee from the U.S.S.R, in a refugee camp in Rome, Italy, growing up in a working class town in New Jersey, going to NYU, going to Oxford, going to the University of London, becoming a licensed attorney, being elected as a Councilman in Englewood Cliffs, a Police Commissioner, an Author, a father, my favorite, owning his own law firm, being healthy, content, and being a master of my own destiny. One in a million, and maybe higher, is it genetics, moral luck, intelligence, guts, timing, my looks (probably not), funny part, I have not even started, first 50 have been good, the next 50 are going to be even better. I especially want to thank Aurelie Binisti who is the love of my life and partner and has given me the inspiration to live, love and dream again from the Hamptons, Pebble Beach, Beverly Hills, Paris, Capri, Positano, and Napoli and Nice, France on July 21, 2022 through 108!

That is the Blueprint, a recipe for destruction, if they do not give you heaven, raise hell! And always remember bended knee is no way to be free!!!

Made in the USA
Monee, IL
05 November 2026

67385063R00052